HEY DOC,
I've Got a Question...

Author: Charles Fischbein, M.D.   Illustrator: Robyn Levine

Text copyright © 2013 by Charles Fischbein
Illustrations copyright © 2013 by Robyn Levine

All rights reserved. No part of the book may be reproduced or transmitted in any form or by any means, electronic or mechanical, including photocopying, recording, or by any information storage retreival system, without permission in writing from the publisher.

Design by Robyn Levine

Library of Congress Cataloging-in-publication Data
Fischbein, Charles
Hey Doc, I Have a Question
ISBN-13: 978-0615738482 (Hey Doc, I Have a Question)

ISBN-10: 0615738486

Introduction

Pediatrics is a wonderful profession. I get to see children of all ages at their worst and at their best. I also get to work with some wonderful parents. I have learned over the years that if you keep your eyes and ears open you can see and hear some amazing things; some of those things are so humorous they must be retold. This book is based on some humorous telephone exchanges with my office, some of which seem unlikely. Believe me, you can't make this stuff up. These are a few of the most enjoyable calls. I hope this brings a smile to your face as it does to mine.

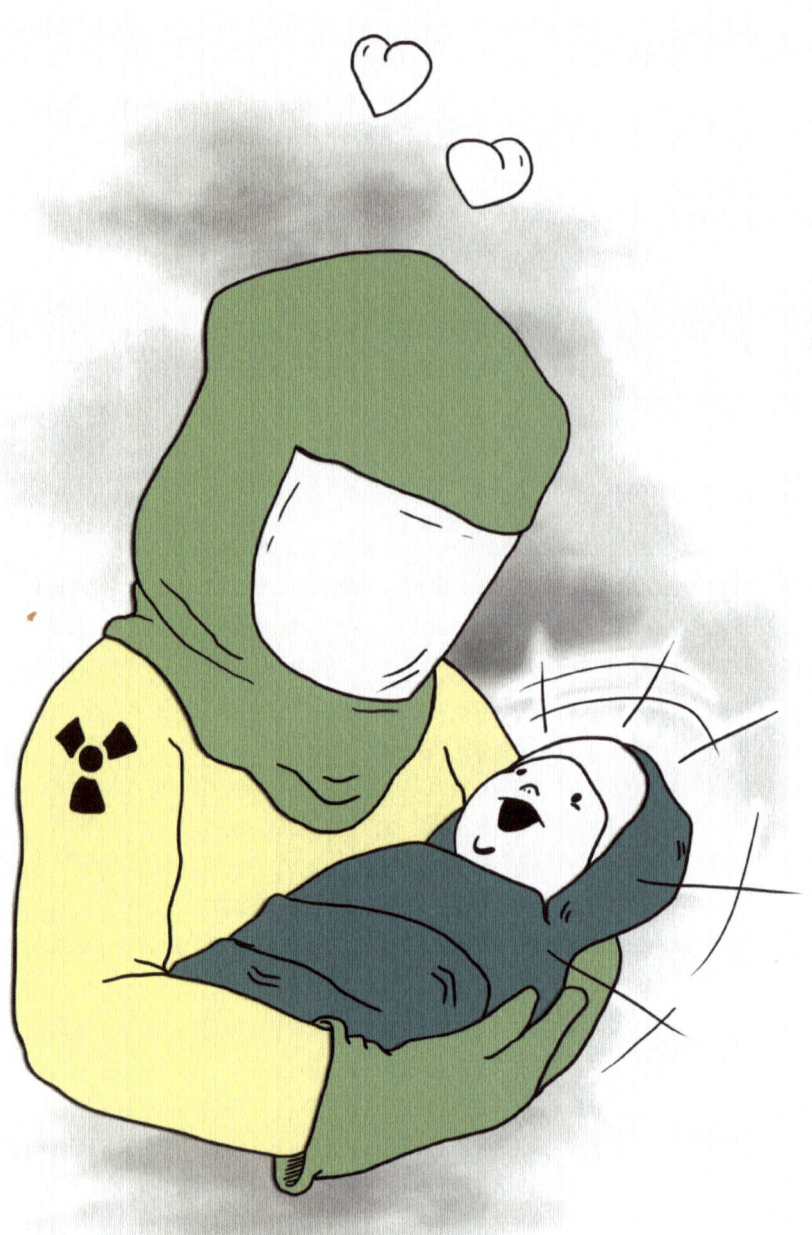

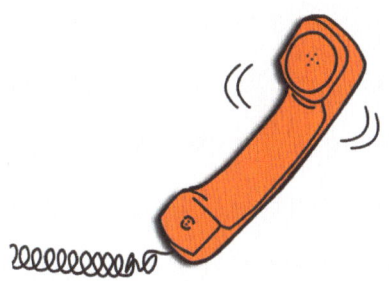

PHONE MEMO

MESSAGE:

Mother: Hi, I want to know if my new insurance will cover my son's last visit.

Office: Is your insurance retroactive for your son?

Mother: He's been radioactive for six months.

PHONED	CALL BACK	RETURNED CALL	WANTS TO SEE YOU	WILL CALL AGAIN	WAS IN	URGENT

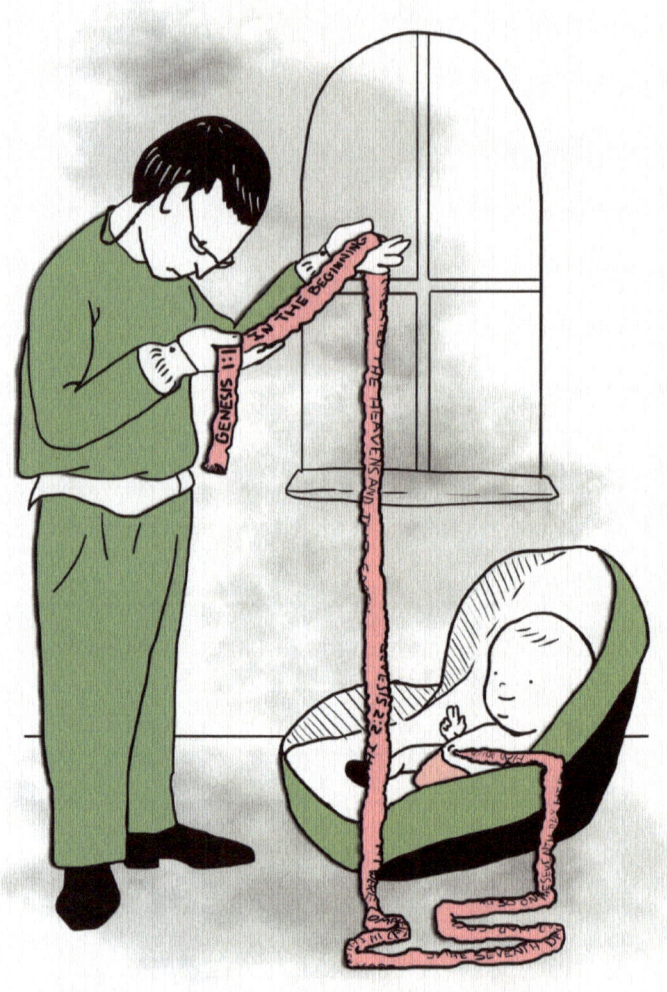

P H O N E M E M O	Office: Can I help you?						
	Father: Yes, we have a new baby. How do we care for the unbiblical cord?						
	M E S S A G E						
	PHONED	CALL BACK	RETURNED CALL	WANTS TO SEE YOU	WILL CALL AGAIN	WAS IN	URGENT

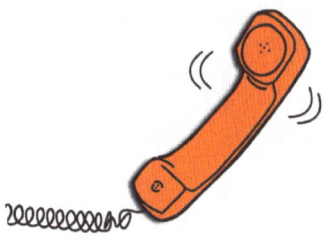

PHONE MEMO

MESSAGE: Father: Hi. I have an animal question. Do hermit crabs carry rabies and can you get sick from handling them?

PHONED | CALL BACK | RETURNED CALL | WANTS TO SEE YOU | WILL CALL AGAIN | WAS IN | URGENT

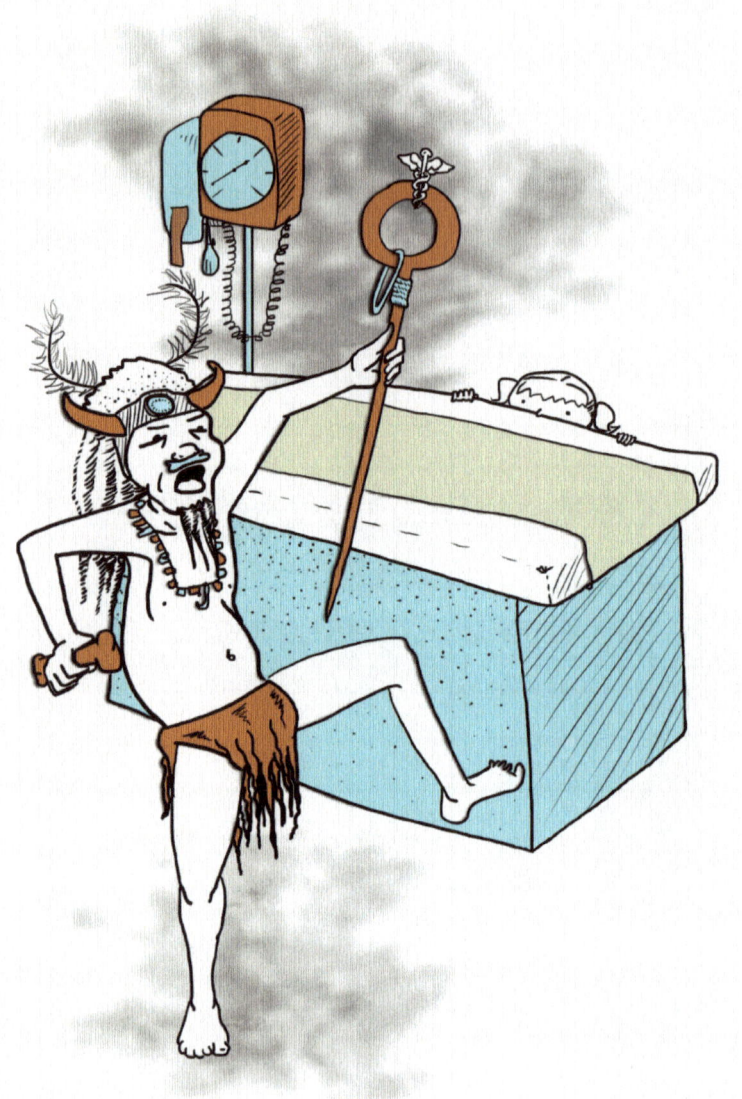

PHONE MEMO	Office: Which doctor would you like your daughter to see?						
	Mother: Gee, we've never seen the witch doctor.						
	MESSAGE						
	PHONED	CALL BACK	RETURNED CALL	WANTS TO SEE YOU	WILL CALL AGAIN	WAS IN	URGENT

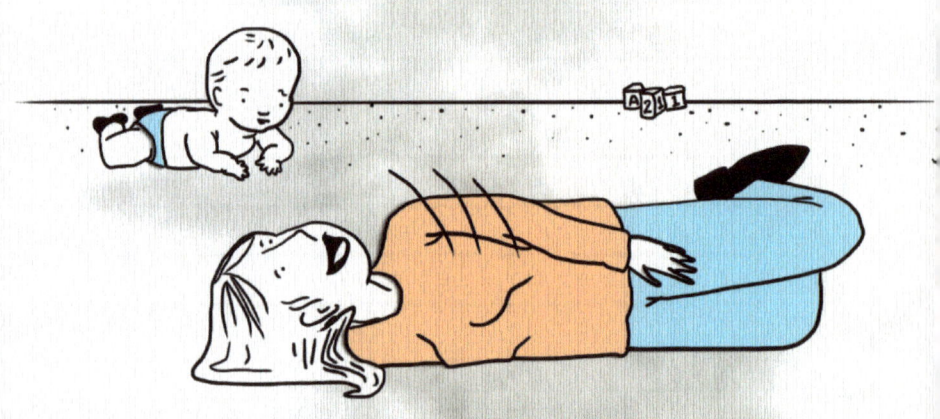

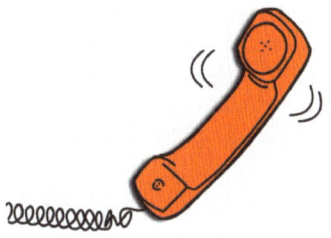

PHONE MEMO	Mother: Hi, I have a development question.
	Office: Yes?
	Mother: How do I teach my four month old to roll over?

PHONED	CALL BACK	RETURNED CALL	WANTS TO SEE YOU	WILL CALL AGAIN	WAS IN	URGENT

PHONE MEMO

MESSAGE

Office: Does your daughter have a fever?
Mother: I don't know. My terminator is broken.

| PHONED | CALL BACK | RETURNED CALL | WANTS TO SEE YOU | WILL CALL AGAIN | WAS IN | URGENT |

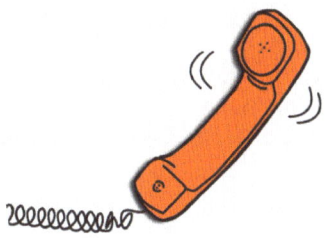

PHONE MEMO		Office: So your son has diarrhea and vomiting?	
		Father: Yes. If he gets dehydrated should we throw him in the pool?	
	MESSAGE		
	PHONED	CALL BACK	RETURNED CALL	WANTS TO SEE YOU	WILL CALL AGAIN	WAS IN	URGENT

PHONE MEMO		Office: Why can't you bring your child to the Waterbury office?
		Mother: Well his father is brain damaged and can only drive in Southbury.
	MESSAGE	
PHONED	CALL BACK	RETURNED CALL	WANTS TO SEE YOU	WILL CALL AGAIN	WAS IN	URGENT

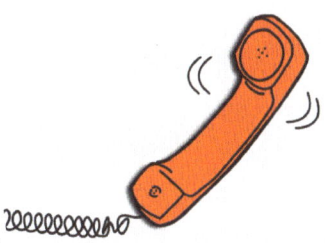

PHONE MEMO	MESSAGE	Office: Since you were in a motor vehicle accident, can I ask if your child had a seat belt on?
		Mother: No he did not. He was in his bed when the car came through the wall
PHONED	CALL BACK	RETURNED CALL	WANTS TO SEE YOU	WILL CALL AGAIN	WAS IN	URGENT

PHONE MEMO		Mother: My child was poked in the eye on the playground and since then refuses to open it.
	MESSAGE	Office: Would you like her to be seen?
		Mother: Yes. Do you think there is any way her eye could have fallen out?

PHONED	CALL BACK	RETURNED CALL	WANTS TO SEE YOU	WILL CALL AGAIN	WAS IN	URGENT

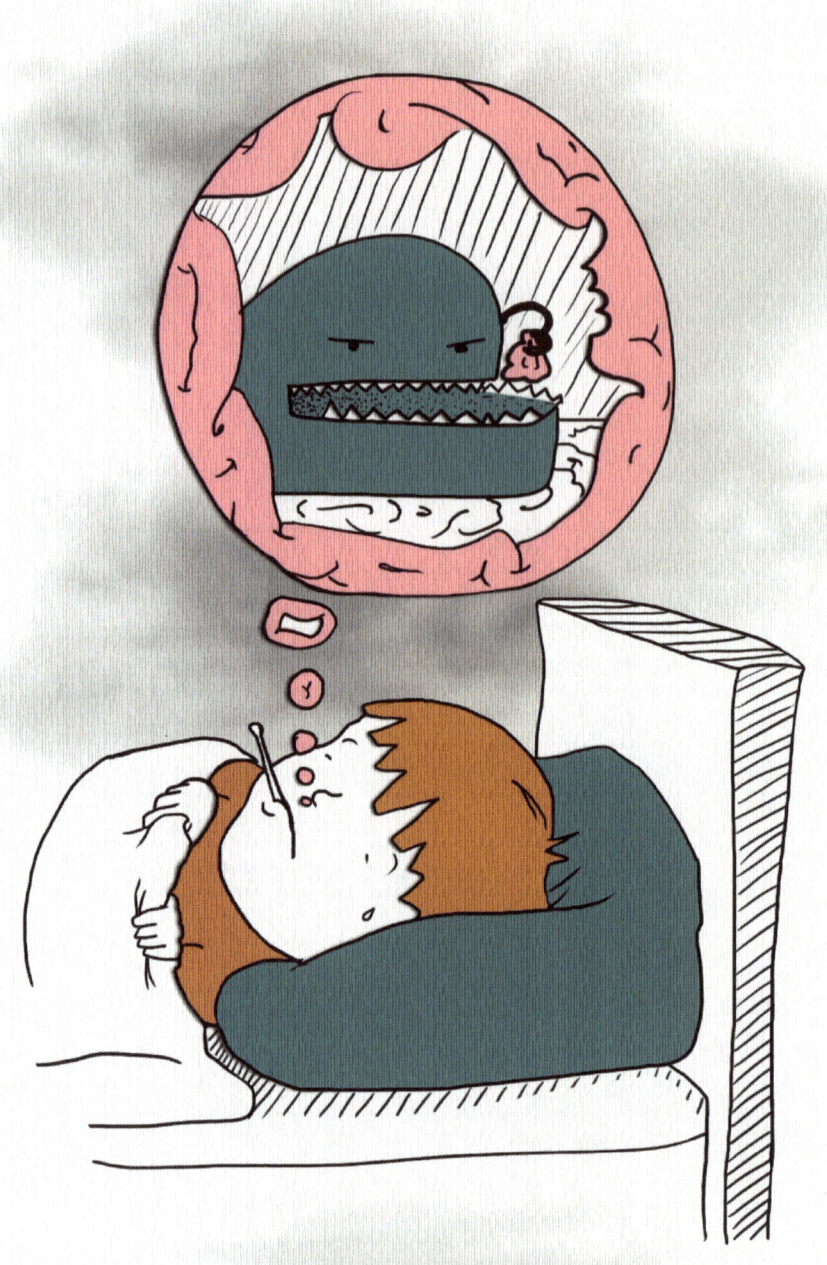

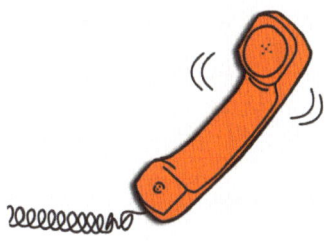

PHONE MEMO	MESSAGE	Office: So your 10 year old son has a fever of 101.2?
		Mother: Yes, and he also feels woozy.
		I'm concerned he has a parasite that has
		crawled up his nose and is eating his
		brain.

PHONED	CALL BACK	RETURNED CALL	WANTS TO SEE YOU	WILL CALL AGAIN	WAS IN	URGENT

PHONE MEMO	MESSAGE	Office: May I help you?
		Mother: Yes. Is it OK to crush my son's vitamins to put in his shampoo to try to increase his hair growth? His grandmother thinks if I do that he might grow small breasts on his scalp.

PHONED	CALL BACK	RETURNED CALL	WANTS TO SEE YOU	WILL CALL AGAIN	WAS IN	URGENT

ACKNOWLEDGEMENTS

This book has been in the planning stage for most of my 39 years of Pediatric practice. It would never have happened without the constant encouragement and support of my wonderful wife of 44 years, Ellen. This one's for you. Over the years I have been blessed to work with many terrific triage nurses. They diligently kept track of these calls and were forced to keep a straight face when others would have been rolling on the floor. My sincere gratitude goes to Cyndi, Maria, Kim, Debbie, Danielle, Joan, Wendy, Monica, Erin, Bobbi, Jaime, Sherry and all those who came before them. A little humor in the work place is a good thing.
A lot is even better.

CAF Waterbury, 2013

www.ingramcontent.com/pod-product-compliance
Lightning Source LLC
Chambersburg PA
CBHW041756040426
42446CB00001B/59